anythink

D0787700

anythink

Journey of the
HUMMINGBIRDS

BY ANNERENEÈ GOYETTE

Gareth Stevens
PUBLISHING

Please visit our website, www.garethstevens.com. For a free color catalog of all our high-quality books, call toll free 1-800-542-2595 or fax 1-877-542-2596.

Cataloging-in-Publication Data

Names: Goyette, AnneReneé.
Title: Journey of the hummingbirds / AnneReneé Goyette.
Description: New York : Gareth Stevens Publishing, 2019. | Series: Massive animal migrations | Includes index.
Identifiers: ISBN 9781538216422 (pbk.) | ISBN 9781538216415 (library bound) | ISBN 9781538216439 (6 pack)
Subjects: LCSH: Hummingbirds--Juvenile literature.
Classification: LCC QL696.A558 G69 2018 | DDC 598.7'64--dc23

First Edition

Published in 2019 by
Gareth Stevens Publishing
111 East 14th Street, Suite 349
New York, NY 10003

Copyright © 2019 Gareth Stevens Publishing

Designer: Katelyn E. Reynolds
Editor: Joan Stoltman

Photo credits: Cover, p. 1 cglade/E+/Getty Images; cover, pp. 1–24 (background) Vadim Georgiev/Shutterstock.com; cover, pp. 1–24 (background) CS Stock/Shutterstock.com; p. 5 KellyNelson/Shutterstock.com; p. 7 Henner Damke/Shutterstock.com; p. 9 Peter Dang/Shutterstock.com; p. 11 Danita Delimont/Gallo Images/Getty Images; p. 13 Jeremy Borkat/Shutterstock.com; p. 15 George D. Lepp/Corbis Documentary/Getty Images; pp. 17, 19 (map) Serban Bogdan/Shutterstock.com; p. 17 (hummingbird) Birdiegal/Shutterstock.com; p. 19 (hummingbird) Paul Tessier/Shutterstock.com; p. 21 Ed Sweeney/Moment/Getty Images.

All rights reserved. No part of this book may be reproduced in any form without permission in writing from the publisher, except by a reviewer.

Printed in the United States of America

CPSIA compliance information: Batch #CS18GS: For further information contact Gareth Stevens, New York, New York at 1-800-542-2595.

CONTENTS

WORDS IN THE GLOSSARY APPEAR IN **BOLD** TYPE
THE FIRST TIME THEY ARE USED IN THE TEXT.

The Tiniest Bird
IN THE WORLD

Hummingbirds are quite amazing creatures. They're the tiniest birds in the world. In fact, they're the tiniest **warm-blooded** animals, weighing in at less than the weight of two dimes! Hummingbirds can beat their wings so fast that they hover in place and can stop instantly. They can also fly directly up, down, or backward!

There are almost 340 species, or kinds, of hummingbirds in the world. Only 17 species **migrate** to the United States. Those migrators return to the same exact plants every year.

Hummingbirds are important! When a hummingbird gets near a flower to eat, pollen sticks to its body. It carries that pollen to the next flower it visits!

5

Migrating TO EAT

A hummingbird's life is all about eating. It's why they migrate!

To eat, a hummingbird hovers in front of a flower, flapping its wings over 50 times a second. Its heart beats 1,260 times a minute to move blood and **oxygen** to its special chest **muscles**. This keeps them from tiring! Hummingbird tongues have two long grooves, or hollows. These grooves fill with nectar inside a flower as they lick 20 times a second. When they pull their tongue back in, the nectar is **squeezed** out and down their throat.

> **THERE'S MORE!**
>
> HUMMINGBIRDS FLY LOW DURING DAYLIGHT WHILE MIGRATING SO THEY CAN SEE FLOWERS. THEY MAY STOP TO EAT FOR A FEW MINUTES OR A FEW DAYS AT A TIME.

Hummingbirds can see more colors and from farther away than people can. They use their awesome eyes to find flowers, especially those that are red, orange, and yellow!

Eating to MIGRATE

Spring migration begins when the days start to get longer where hummingbirds live. These seasonal changes mean the end of blooming flowers in one place and the beginning of blooming flowers in another. It's time to fly!

Before a migration, hummingbirds eat their weight in nectar plus about 2,000 tiny bugs—filled with fat and **protein**—every day! This much eating doubles their weight. The fat they gain is stored evenly throughout their body so they can still fly well.

THERE'S MORE!

NECTAR HAS SUGAR. BUGS HAVE PROTEINS AND FAT. FAT IS IMPORTANT TO EAT BEFORE A MIGRATION BECAUSE IT HAS THE MOST **ENERGY**! NOT EATING ENOUGH FAT BEFORE A MIGRATION CAN MEAN DEATH!

9

Food, GLORIOUS FOOD!

After migration, hummingbirds get right back to eating! They arrive just in time to see the flowers blooming. They spend all day eating, **digesting**, or searching for food. Hummingbirds need to eat a lot because they use an incredible amount of energy. They burn through up to three times their body weight in food energy every day!

Hummingbirds leave a feeding area when the flowers are almost done blooming. They may even change their migration's timing if blooming patterns change!

THERE'S MORE!

HUMMINGBIRDS DON'T FLY UNLESS THEY NEED TO CHASE OFF SOMEONE OR FEED. EVEN THE SMALLEST AMOUNT OF FLYING CAN KILL THEM IF THEY DON'T FIND ENOUGH FOOD EVERY SINGLE DAY!

Because hummingbirds beat their wings the entire time they're flying, their body burns through lots of energy. In fact, they burn through energy 100 times faster than an elephant!

TORPOR

Since hummingbirds can travel as far as 23 miles (37 km) in a day, migration is very tiring. Hovering to eat requires a ton of energy, so even days they aren't migrating are exhausting. What's a hummingbird to do?

Hummingbirds enter a state called torpor every night to save energy. In torpor, they drop the **temperature** of their body nearly 50°F (10°C) and slow their heart and breathing. Without torpor, they could lose 10 percent of their body weight working to keep warm!

THERE'S MORE!

HUMMINGBIRDS MUST HIDE DEEP IN TREES DURING SLEEP. IT CAN TAKE THEM AN HOUR OF SHIVERING TO GET THEIR BLOOD FLOWING ENOUGH TO FULLY WAKE UP FROM TORPOR.

Hummingbirds lock their feet onto a branch during torpor.

locked feet

NESTLINGS

Hummingbirds also migrate to **breed.** Males travel first to claim their territories. Females follow, building nests soon after arriving. Males leave after breeding. Females then care for the eggs and nestlings, or baby hummingbirds. Females catch small bugs so the nestlings get protein to grow. Their favorite bugs include flies, small bees, spiders, and caterpillars.

Hummingbird hatchlings begin flying around 20 days after birth. Most die their first year, as these tiny creatures are food for larger birds, cats, mice, dragonflies, frogs, and fish.

> ## THERE'S MORE!
> FEMALE HUMMINGBIRDS ARE 15 TO 20 PERCENT LARGER THAN MALES. THEY NEED THE EXTRA SIZE TO PRODUCE EGGS, SHARE BODY HEAT WITH EGGS, AND SHARE FOOD WITH NESTLINGS.

Hummingbird eggs are the size of jelly beans, and nests are the size of walnut shells. Females gather leafy matter, bark, and moss for their nests and then hold it all together with spider webbing!

15

The Rufous
HUMMINGBIRD

The rufous hummingbird makes the longest bird migration in the world for its body size. At 3 inches (7.6 cm) long, its nearly 4,000-mile (6,400 km) journey is 84 million times the length of its tiny body!

Rufous hummingbirds spend winter in Mexico and the United States along the Gulf of Mexico. They migrate up the Pacific coast in spring along a path called the "floral highway" because of all the flowers. By summer, they've made it to the Pacific Northwest and even Alaska!

>< THERE'S MORE! ><

RUFOUS HUMMINGBIRDS START AND END THE DAY EATING AT THE EDGES OF THEIR TERRITORY. THE REST OF THE DAY IS SPENT ATTACKING ANYONE WHO GETS TOO CLOSE TO THEIR TERRITORY, INCLUDING CHIPMUNKS AND BIRDS TWICE THEIR SIZE!

RUFOUS HUMMINGBIRD MIGRATION

ALASKA

CANADA

□ breeding

□ migration

□ non-breeding

UNITED STATES

Pacific Ocean

MEXICO

rufous hummingbird

17

The Ruby-Throated
HUMMINGBIRD

The ruby-throated hummingbird has the largest breeding range of any North American hummingbird! That's because it's the only hummingbird to go to the East Coast.

Ruby-throated hummingbirds spend winter in Central America, southern Mexico, and on the Gulf Coast. The most amazing thing about their migration is that they cross the Gulf of Mexico! This trip takes 18 to 24 hours of flying nonstop, depending on weather. They arrive exhausted and hungry. Some don't arrive at all if they didn't gain enough weight before migrating.

THERE'S MORE!

RUBY-THROATED HUMMINGBIRDS HEAD NORTH BEGINNING IN FEBRUARY. THE LATER THEY LEAVE IN SPRING, THE FARTHER NORTH THEY'LL FLY.

In good weather, the ruby-throated hummingbird can fly 600 miles (965 km) without stopping. The flight across the Gulf of Mexico is only 500 miles (805 km)!

RUBY-THROATED HUMMINGBIRD MIGRATION

CANADA

UNITED
STATES

MEXICO

Gulf of
Mexico

Atlantic
Ocean

summer
migration
winter

ruby-throated
hummingbird

Hummingbirds NEED HELP!

Scientists are learning more about hummingbird migrations than ever before thanks to new **technology**! They finally have tools tiny enough to fix to the birds so they can track migrations.

But scientists only have a rough idea of where and when hummingbirds travel. We can't keep hummingbirds safe if we don't know where they go! Rufous hummingbirds are especially in danger because of ever-growing cities and **climate change.** Hopefully we can do something to keep these amazing birds around for years to come!

21

GLOSSARY

breed: to come together to make babies

climate change: long-term change in Earth's climate, caused partly by human activities

digest: to change food that has been eaten into simpler forms that can be used by the body

energy: power used to do work

migrate: to move to warmer or colder places for a season for feeding or having babies

muscle: one of the parts of the body that allow movement

oxygen: a colorless, odorless gas that many animals, including people, need to breathe

protein: a nutrient found in many types of food that the body uses to grow and repair itself

squeeze: to press something tightly

technology: the way people do something using tools and the tools that they use

temperature: how hot or cold something is

warm-blooded: able to keep the body at a steady temperature no matter what the outside temperature is

FOR MORE INFORMATION

Books

Bader, Bonnie. *Hummingbirds*. New York, NY: Grosset & Dunlap, 2015.

Berne, Emma Carlson. *Hummingbirds: Faster Than a Jet!* New York, NY: PowerKids Press, 2014.

Bogue, Gary. *There's a Hummingbird in My Backyard*. Berkeley, CA: Heyday Books, 2010.

Websites

Go Mobile with Journey North
learner.org/jnorth/mobile/index.html
Journey North is an app that lets you be a citizen scientist. Report your migration sightings from the field!

West Texas Hummingbirds
cams.allaboutbirds.org/channel/50/West_Texas_Hummingbirds/
Watch a live video of hummingbirds in Fort Davis, Texas, feeding right now!

Publisher's note to educators and parents: Our editors have carefully reviewed these websites to ensure that they are suitable for students. Many websites change frequently, however, and we cannot guarantee that a site's future contents will continue to meet our high standards of quality and educational value. Be advised that students should be closely supervised whenever they access the Internet.

INDEX